GOD OF MANKIND

Luthando Ningiza

Copyright ©2020 Luthando Ningiza

ISBN: 978-1-990940-13-2

First Published in 2020 by Celenic Earth Publications, Cape Town, SOUTH AFRICA

All Rights Reserved. All opinions in this book are of the author.

No part of this eBook, whether text or images created by the author for the purposes of this book, may be reproduced or transmitted in any form or by any means, electronic or mechanical, including photocopying, recording or by any information storage and retrieval system, without written permission from the author.

Other Works by Author:

Greatness of God

TABLE OF CONTENTS

A) Dedication   i
B) Acknowledgement   ii
C) Introduction   v
D) References   vi

1) Maintain Your Life With God   1
2) The Battle is the Lord's   28
3) Help Is At Hand   50
4) Be Cautious   77
5) Commit To The Lord   98

DEDICATION

I would like to dedicate this book to all those who are facing struggles in their lives. Those who think there is no future hope for them. You know what my Brother my Sister, it's not like what you see in this world; there is more to it than what you think. For you to discover that and see the best the Lord have for you, come closer to God.

He is the God of mankind. He will never live you nor forsake you. His mercies are new every day!

ACKNOWLEDGEMENT

My sincere and grateful special thanks, appreciation and acknowledgement goes to:

*First and foremost, I would like to thank my **Lord** my **God** in *Jesus Christ's* name, who gave me the mind and the Idea of a vision to start writing, and thank You Lord my God. You kept on pouring in me and revealing in me what I should say and deliver to your people by writing it down. I didn't have an Idea of what I should write about and what I should do, but you stood there by my side and kept on pouring to me what I should write it down, up to the end of this book. You were with me all the way. *Thank you, God my Lord!*

* **My local Church Pastor, Mr Mjongisi Mpotololo.** I don't have the perfect words to say to you. I am deeply humbled and honoured to have you in my life. Your support, motivation and prayers played a vital role in my life. Truly, you are that leader and that father that is expected. To you "Yes is Yes", "No is No". You never compromised the truth of the Lord in order to please people. Thank you so much, I'm glad that God brought you closer to my life. You truly showed and displayed the signs of a real Shepherd. **"Look, there on the mountains, the feet of one who brings good news, who proclaims peace!"** {Nahum1: 15}

*To my Dearest important people in my life. Who made me to realise who I am, and made me to have a sense of belonging and a knowledge of knowing that I matter? Without them, I have no Idea what my life would be. My mother whom I love and admire very much, **Dokazi Lydia Ningiza,** my brother **Anele** and my sister **Yonela Ningiza**, and my children; my son **Reyaoboka** familiarly known as **"Reya"** **Rankutu** and my daughter **Mandilive** also familiarly known as *"Live* **" Mavume**. Mr **Bulela Nonkonyana**, whom I take and consider him as my little younger brother.

Thanks for all the time and space you gave me to sit down and write this book without disturbing me, until the day I finished it. May God my Lord be with them at all times.

*The **Pambo** family, my Aunt family, at Ezibeleni township Queenstown. Ku-Komani.
Mr.Mxolisi Robert Pambo, Mrs.Nokhaya "Sis'Ntombi" Maureen Pambo. Their children, the late **Zukiswa {RIP} ; Lizo,Nelisa & Mfundo Pambo.** Also I can't forget my aunt **Nombulelo Gladys Ningiza**, her children for their love and support.

I have tried to measure the Length, Width, Breadth, Depth and Height of your Love, Support and almost everything you have done for me. It's totally unmeasurable.
{Matthew 25:35-40} take note of verse"40"; You did exactly as the scriptures command. I thank you. God Bless you all in Christ Jesus!

*I sincerely couldn't stop thanking God for the following people, who never turned their back away from me; they were so close to me, in thick and hard times.
Whenever I think back of the things you have done for me, I feel and became emotional up to the point that I feel I am going to cry tears. You didn't know me, you met with me here in Cape Town with God's grace. Truly to me you played the role of a brother to lean on. You have truly fulfilled the scriptures when they say:

"Love One Another"
"This is my command: Love each other" {John15:17}, you guys; You have done that.

Thank You!

1) Mr. Danny Mpumelelo Mbanyana and his family.
2) Mr. Avumile Agreement Sinaba and his family.
3) Mr. James Makeleni and his family.

*People who gave all their assistance and help for me to manage up to the end of publishing and seeing to it that it is out there to the market reaching its target. Thanks for your time and every effort you have done for me.

*Audience at large-you people who will be buying and reading this book and spreading the word of God to the world at large and reach where the Gospel of Christ the Lord the Messiah is not preached. I Love you and highly appreciate your support. {*Hamba Vangeli*}

INTRODUCTION

About the Book

The book contains a message that tries to show and reveals an awesome, incredible love of God towards mankind. Provided a man puts it into practice, what is written in the Bible as it is illustrated here in the book.

With God and You; you two can work wonders as you walk miles together.

Yes it's true; we can't control the wind, the rain or the other vagaries of weather. But we can tack our sails so that we can steer the course we desire.

The Aims of the Book

The aim is for each individual to create an action plan in their Spiritual lives. By doing so, they will be providing the blueprint or map of their spirituality which will lead them towards the culminating of their dreams. Spiritual people should realize this and be prepared to invest their time for their spirituality, doing the most important things first and the least important next.

REFERENCES:

All Bible verses were quoted from:
NIV BIBLE AND **HOLY BIBLE.** {King James Version}

GOD OF MANKIND

Maintain Your Life With God

There are not many things in this life that you can count on, but two are always being there and always being the same. What is it that you can think of, that is constant sure and steady?

People come and go, their loyalty and love end and flow, jobs disappear, and situations change.

That word 'change', it's not constant in life. Well if there can be nothing constant and things keep on changing because of the changing times and situations. Then you have to look again and seek and find out what is it that you need to do in order to get to the point of getting to that constant unchanging person in this world.

Then, that person is nobody else but God the Lord the creator Himself. For God is one person that you can always count on and maintain your life with, in this world we are living in it and the ever eternity.

He is always present and always the same today, tomorrow and forever. His character is steady. He is not dependent on moods or situations. You know him through His word and through your past experiences with him, and when you deeply think way back, and the things you have passed through.

You don't stop asking yourself, how did you managed to get over and passed all that. You will realise that it is not by your wisdom or what, it is all by his wonderful grace. So you know him by his character; unlike a human being, He will never act contrary to who he is, He is always having your best interest in his heart.

The best way to maintain your life with God the creator is to know that He is the anchor to hang on in everything in life. He who is the glory of Israel does not lie, nor a son of man that he should change his mind.

Does He speak then not act? Does He promise and not fulfil?

"**God is not a man, that he should lie, nor a son of man, that he should change his mind. Does he speak and then not act?** " {Numbers 23:19}

"**For the Lord is good and his love endure forever, his faithfulness continues through all generations**" {Psalm 100:5}

So to maintain your unshakable life with God is to be in Christ Jesus, to attain His Love by being obedient to Him.

"**As the Father has loved me, so have I loved you. Now remain in my love** " {John 15:9}.

To maintain your life with God can be divided into three categories:

LOVE

FAITH

OBEDIENCE

If you can master the three categories. Surely you will have a strong relationship with God, and you have to maintain that standard with God in Christ Jesus.

Then Who or What, can separate you from the Lord?

"Who shall separate us from the Love of Christ, shall tribulation, or distress, or persecution, or famine or nakedness or peril or sword" & 37- **"Nay, in all these things we are more than conquers through him that loved us"** {Romans 8:35&37}

A dot becomes a line, a line becomes a shape, a shape becomes a pattern, a pattern becomes an artwork. One must always remember to start at the pure basics.

In the end, you will end up with a masterpiece.

<u>LOVE</u>

<u>WHAT IS IT?</u>

It is the inner feeling that gives peace and harmony in someone's lives and the surroundings. The feeling that wants and strives for the best out of the best.

A true realistic feeling that doesn't change, because of the changing times or situations; it's a strong affection. It is the feeling that travels and reflects God, because God is Love. It is the single most powerful and necessary component in life. It is the foundation of all relations.

It is the sacred reserve of energy; it is like the blood of spiritual evolution.

Love is a verb, an action word, not a noun. There are people who say, love is blind. Whoever says so, is dead wrong. Love is the only thing that let us see each other with the remotest accuracy.

ITS IMPORTANCE

Let us see how important love is to God and how our life can be maintained with God through love. To maintain a relationship with God, you have to be filled with love towards Him and others.

Love establishes a reliable base on which bonding can build. The soul grows well when giving and receiving love. Love conquers multitude of sins; people can hurt you, disappoint you, due to love. You will find them forgiveness in your heart; that will make you pure in your heart all because of the power of love. Love make you sincere, and hate what is evil and to cling to what is good.

"Let love be without dissimulation. Abhor that which is evil; cleave to that which is good. Be kindly affected one

to another with brotherly love; in honour preferring one another" {Romans12:9-10}

Love makes us patient, understanding and kind. And we judge with our heart and mind not with our eyes. For as soon as love enters heart's open door, the faults we once saw are not there anymore.

That fulfils the scriptures when it says, love covers multitude of sins.

"**Above all, love each other deeply, because love covers over a multitude of sins**"
{1Peter4:8}

WHEN LOVING

When loving, the more you seek and communicate with God, it's the more you grow zeal and passion for worshipping and serving Him. It is the more you love others unconditional and equally, you don't categorise and standardise God's people. You feel it deep down inside of you.

"If I speak in the tongues of men and of angels, but have not love, I am only a resounding gong or a clanging cymbal."

{1Corinthains13:1}

"Owe no man anything, but to love one another: for he that loved another hath fulfilled the law." {Romans 13:8} and;

"Dear friends, since God so loved us, we also ought to love one another, & We love because he first loved us. If anyone says, "I love God," yet hates his brother, he is the liar. For anyone who does not love his brother, whom he has seen, cannot love God, whom he has not seen" {1John 4:11 & 19-20}

LOVE BY ACTIONS

When loving, you don't just say or claim you love, or you have the love, you show it by actions.

"*Actions speaks louder than words.*"

"If I then, your Lord and Teacher, have washed your feet, you also ought to wash anothers feet. For I have given you an example, that you should do as I done to you." {John 13:14-15}

It's no wonder we see how God loved the world, he didn't just claim that he loves it; He showed it by giving up his only begotten son, to save it.

What about you?

When was the last time that you gave to the needy out there in the street? I mean cooking that hot soup and giving those blankets in that cold winter rain?

I mean buying shoes for that needy child in the street and you do that without expecting anything in return?

Mmmm… I got you!

Well you have to repent, and do what is good and right for you to do for others.

"The King will reply, 'I tell you the truth, whatever you did for one of the least of these brothers of mine, you did it for me". {Matthew 25:40}

Can you see? Action! But you all do that out of Love.

Yes action; God did not just claim to love His people, He showed it.

"For God so loved the world, that he gave his only begotten Son, that whosoever Believeth in him should not perish, but have everlasting life." {John 3:16}

and

"Do everything in love" {1Corinthians 16:14}

You can be whatever you are, or you can do whatever you can, but if you don't have love you are just nothing to God. Surely it means that you have not maintained your life with God. When we do things out of great love, rather than great expectation, more comes back to us than we could ever imagined.

All the flowers, of all the tomorrows, are in the seeds of today.

Our days are identical suitcases, all the same size, but some people can pack more into them than others. You can prophecy and fathom mysteries, have faith that moves mountains, but without love, you are nothing.

"And now these three remain: faith, hope, and love. But the greatest of these is love." {1Corinthians 13:13}

If you are the man that claims to be living by the Spirit of the Lord, you should not be lacking in Love, as the love forms the part of the fruits of the Spirit.

"But the fruits of the Spirit is love, joy, peace, patience, kindness, goodness, faithfulness, gentleness and self-control. Against such things there is no law" {Galatians 5:22-23}

Love is the command that we should obey.

"This is my command: Love each other" {John 15:17}

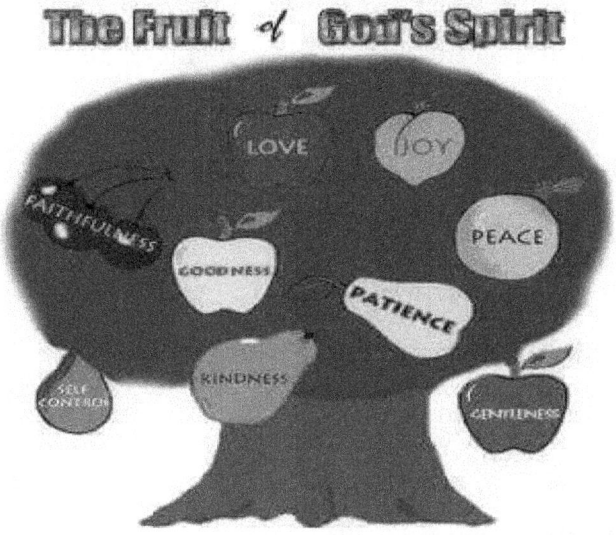

FAITH

I have been watching and listening to sportsmen and women, who have successfully achieved a lot, up to Gold medals and awards in their endeavours. What I heard to what led them to their success, it's nothing else but determination and hard work.

Champions did not just become champions when they won the event. But it took them hours, weeks, months and years, they spend preparing for it.

The victorious performance itself is merely the demonstration of their championship character. To be more positive and being faithful to what they do. They gave themselves wholeheartedly to what they do.

History has demonstrated that the most notable winners usually encountered heart-breaking obstacles before they have triumphed.

They won because they refused to become discouraged by their defeats. So as you, to maintain your life in the Lord, you need to give yourself wholeheartedly. And if what you do, you do without faith, you cannot maintain your life with God, because God won't be pleased with you.

"And without faith it is impossible to please God, because anyone who comes to him must believe that he exists and that he rewards those who earnestly seek him." {Hebrews11:6}

WHAT IS FAITH?

Faith is the anchor that holds your beliefs steady. It is the awareness that the Creator is running the world and all that happens is for your ultimate benefit. The more faith you have, the more you will find yourself experiencing greater degrees of inner peace and serenity.

Faith is seeing the invisible; action is seizing the invisible. Faith without action makes you a dreamer. Action without faith makes you a doer, whereas faith with action makes you an achiever.

Faith sees the invisible, feels the intangible, and achieves the impossible.

Without faith your Christianity is meaningless, prayer is pointless and your relationship with God has no solid foundation.

Faith is the verb that gives an action to all things. It is the gift from God that may start small in your heart, but as you exercise that faith, it grows and grows and brings you closer and closer to God.

"Now faith is being sure of what we hope for and certain of what we do not see." {Hebrews11:1}

"Consequently, faith comes from hearing the message, and the message is heard through the word of Christ." {Romans10:17}

Faith is an anchor in the heart, which can never be reached by the caravan of thinking.

Why the anchor?

The anchor is defined as the heavy object attached to a rope or chain and used to hook a vessel to the sea bottom, typically one having a metal shank with a ring at one end for a rope and a pair of curved or barbed flukes at the ends.

The anchor is used to keep the ship from drifting or pulled away. Therefore, the ship owner rests and puts their hope in their anchor to keep their ship, even in the midst of the biggest storm.

When the storms of life come, when you find they begin to rage the most, Jesus is your sure and steadfast hope. He is as sure and steadfast than even before the storm came. He is the anchor of your soul.

Even when you don't understand it all, trust Him. Like the two curved flukes on an anchor, one side hold God's Promises and the other side also holds His Oaths about you, which He also cannot lie. For God is not a man who can lie.

"God is not a man, that He should lie, Nor a son of man, that He should repent. Has He said, and will He not do? Or has He spoken, and will He not make it good." {Numbers 23: 19 }

So the anchor is a sure consolation, a sure hope that is right there to hold you tight, even at the bottom, your rock bottom. That is what Jesus came for, and there is a hope that you can always look to in Him through your faith.

Jesus went behind the veil, the holiest of the holies, the mercy seat of God and secured salvation for those that received Him. You are not anchored in a sea on earth, but He anchored you up above in Heavenly places.

He won't let you be taken away in the midst of what you are experiencing. Nothing can move what Christ has done. He will keep you through it all. He will carry you through it. For Jesus is really the anchor of your soul. So you have to put all your faith in Him.

ITS IMPORTANCE

Because of faith, we know that God is who He says He is, and that His word is alive and real. You seek to know Him more, to grow deeper in relationship with Him.

Because of faith, you pray to God, believing with all your heart that He hears your prayers and He will answer you. Because of faith, you believe that there is heaven and hell, and it's your choice to determine which of these places will be your eternal home.

Believing in God and accepting Jesus Christ as your saviour, and die to yourself for in Christ Jesus, through your faith, you will strongly maintain your life in the Lord.

"I have been crucified with Christ and I no longer live, but Christ lives in me.

The life I live in the body, I live by faith in the Son of God, who loved me and gave himself for me " {Galatians 2:20}

WORKS OF FAITH

Faith does a total transformation in each and every human life. You become a changed person. You don't remain the same person as you were before.

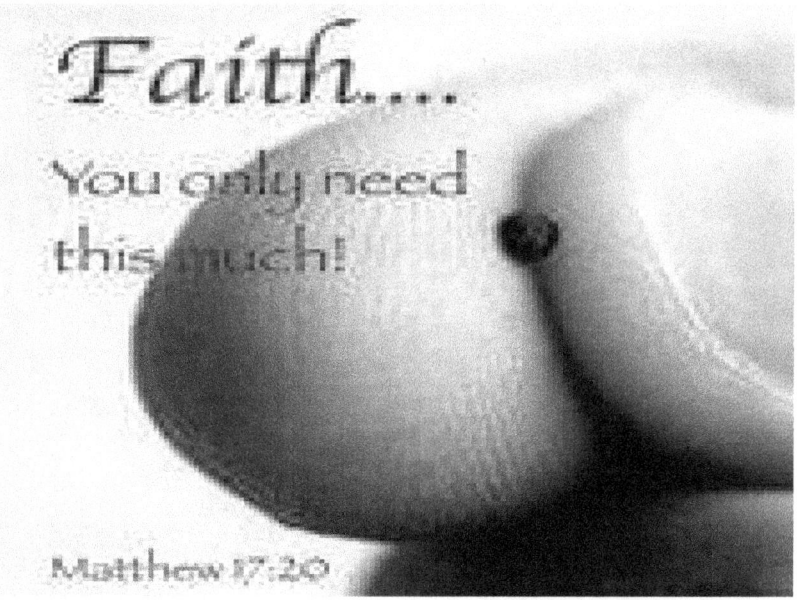

By faith you can be healed, move mountains, and to know God better. It is no wonder why we hear Jesus telling his disciples to have faith as small as a mustard seed.

Why as a mustard seed?

Even though a mustard seed is as small as it is, but it can grow out above the soil and produce a big harvest.

"He replied, "Because you have so little faith. I tell you the truth, if you have faith as small as a mustard seed, you can say to this mountain, 'Move from here to there' and it will move. Nothing will be impossible for you." {Matthew 17:20}

Let us look at these Scenarios, and see how powerful faith works:

First Scenario

The Centurion who had the servant that was sick, did not even bother for Jesus to come himself personal to his house to heal his servant; through the faith that he had within himself, he believed that even if Jesus can just say the word, his servant will be healed. And really the Centurion's servant was really healed.

And Jesus was astonished by the faith of the centurion. That is what we have to do.

To believe him from his word.

"That is why I did not even consider myself worthy to come to you. But say the word, and my servant will be healed "{Luke7:7} and

"When Jesus heard this, he was amazed at him, and turning to the crowd following him he said, "I tell you, I have not found such great faith even in Israel"{Luke7:9}

Second Scenario

And also if you look at the woman who was suffering from bleeding, for twelve years, she deeply told and felt to herself that she doesn't need much for her to be healed by Jesus. But, by the deep strong faith in her heart, she told herself that all she needs is to just to touch Jesus's clothes, and she had a belief that she will be healed.

And we all know what happened. She was really healed and the bleeding stopped.

"Because she thought, "if I just touch his clothes, I will be healed."

{Mark5:28}

Third Scenario

Let us look also at the story of the Israelites, when God asked Moses to send man to go and explore Canaan, which God was going to give it to them. So Moses sent man to go and explore it, they came back with all sorts of negative reports to Moses because of the little faith they had.

But out of all those men, stood up one man, who was full of faith, despite what the situation was and the circumstances they had experienced in Canaan. He stood up and said they can go and take the land. And what happened, with one man's faith, they conquered Canaan.

"Then Caleb silenced the people before Moses and said, "We should go up and take possession of the land, for we can certainly do it." {Numbers 13:30}

Can you see! To all these different case scenarios, they all reveal the power of faith, and how we should have faith in the Lord.

" We live by faith not by sight "
{2Corinthians5:7}

ITS OUTCOMES

Abraham was credited as a righteous man and friend of God, because of his belief and strong faith to God, and the nations and those who have faith were blessed along with Abraham, because he was a man of faith.

"Consider Abraham: "He believed God, and it was credited to him as righteousness. Understand, then, that those who believe are children of Abraham. The Scripture foresaw that God would justify the Gentiles by faith, and announced the gospel in advance to Abraham: "All nations will be blessed through you". So those who have faith are blessed along with Abraham, the man of faith" {Galatians 3:6-9}

CONCLUSION

Why faith is so important to God?

Let us go back to God's creation in the beginning from the book of Genesis1. We will notice that God, whenever he was opening his mouth, that was when he was creating.

He was always saying: ***"Let there be..."***

Whenever God was saying this, he never doubted his words. Those were the words of confidence. He believed and knew what He was saying is going to happen.

He never doubted himself. That is why even to us, He wants us to believe in him, because the belief started with him first, in his words.

That is why He even called Abraham his friend, because Abraham was doing exactly what was expected from him by the Lord. He was faithful to God.

Faith is the key, the access to your breakthrough.

"And without faith it is impossible to please God, because anyone who comes to him must believe that he exists and that he rewards those who earnestly seek him." {Hebrews11:6}

Looking unto Jesus the author and finisher of our faith, who for the joy that was set before him endured the cross, despising the shame, and He is sitting down at the right hand of the throne of God.

"Let us fix our eyes on Jesus, the author and perfecter of our faith, who for the joy set before him endure the cross, scorning its shame, and sat down at the right hand of the throne of God." {Hebrews 12:2}

Olives are *pressed* for oil, fruits are *squeezed* for juice, and flowers are *crushed for* perfumes. These painful processes give value.

So when you feel **Crushed, Squeezed,** and **Pressed**, it's not that it is the end of you. You are getting processed for more better value. Just have strong faith in God, humbling yourself and let yourself be the vessel he wants out of you.

He refines those He love.

OBEDIENCE

WHAT IS IT?

Obedience come through submission and submission is not a subjection or an inferiority. It is a choice that one makes. Christ chose to be submissive and to submit his life to save us. Obedience is chosen out of reverence for Christ.

"Submit to one another out of reverence of Christ." {Ephesians 5:21}

Just like that centurion who not even bothered Jesus to come to his house. But the obedience he had with him, He knew that whatever Jesus will say, He will immediately obey and do it. Without doubts or hesitation.

"For I myself am a man under authority, with soldiers under me. I tell this one, 'Go', and he goes; and that one,' Come' and he comes. I say to my servant, 'Do this', and he does it." {Luke 7:8}.

If you are obedient to God, you don't hesitate. You do immediately as you are commanded by God to do so. Just like the first disciples that were called to follow Jesus, they did not hesitate, they immediately left their nets, boat and their father and followed Jesus.

Can you see the obedience that was in those fisherman's?

"At once they left their nets and followed him" & **"and immediately they left the boat and their father and followed him."** {Matthew 4:20 & 22}

ITS IMPORTANCE

Why is obedience highly important in maintaining your life with God? Obedience is a sign that shows how much you respect the one who is above you and to whatever he is asking you to do.

Obedience is not only for those who are in senior position to you, even to those who are younger to you, when you are obedient to them, you manage to win their respect. Being obedient to God, it is what delights him.

"Does the Lord delight in burnt offerings and sacrifices as much as in obedience to the voice of the Lord? To obey is better than sacrifice, and to heed is better than the fat of rams" {Samuel 15:22}

WORKS OF OBEDIENCE:

Be obedient, draw God closer to yourself, He is there with you, for you. No harm will come closer to you.

"The angel of the Lord encamps around those who fear him, and he delivers them." {Psalm 34:7} and

"Whoever obeys his command will come to no harm, and the wise heart will know the proper time and procedure." {Ecclesiastes 8:5}.

When obedient, you are lifted up high, your foot doesn't strike against a stone, and you tread upon lions and cobra.

"If you make the Most High your dwelling---even the

Lord, who is my refuge--then no harm will come near your tent. For he will command his angels concerning you to guard you in all your ways; they will lift you up in their hands, so that you will not strike your foot against a stone. You will tread upon the lion and the cobra; you will trample the great lion and the serpent " {Psalm91:9-13}

OUTCOMES OF OBEDIENCE

Through obedience, you stand your grounds to what you believe at. You are not shaken.

"But Peter and John replied, "Judge for yourselves whether it is right to obey you rather than God. For we cannot help speaking about what we have seen and heard." {Acts 4:19-20}.

Some of the orders may be challenging and very difficult to obey; they may want to see you moving away from the Lord, if you obey them.

Let us look at the book of Esther, whereby we see Mordecai not kneeling at Haman, who was just given a higher seat of honour by the King, but Modercai didn't bow and kneel down to Haman.

"Then the royal officials at the King's gate asked Mordecai, "Why do you disobey the King's command?" {Esther 3:3}

"Surely he will save you from the fowler's snare and from the pestilence. He will cover you with his feathers, and under his wings you will find refuge; his faithfulness will be your shield and rampart. You will not fear the terror of night, nor the arrow that flies by day, nor the pestilence that stalk in the darkness nor the plague that destroys at midday.

A thousand may fall at your side, ten thousand at your right hand, but it will not come near you. You will only observe with your eyes and see the punishment of the wicked " {Psalm 91:3-8}

Why will you enjoy such a privilege with God my Lord through your obedience?

"Because he loves me, "says the Lord, "I will rescue him; I will protect him, for he acknowledges my name. He will call upon me, and I will answer him; I will be with him in trouble, and I will deliver him and honour him. With long life will I satisfy him and show him my salvation" {Psalm 91:14-16}

The Battle is the Lord's

There is no pain that Jesus can't feel. No Hurt that He can't heal. For all things work according to the master's purpose and His Holy will. No matter what you are going through, remember that God only wants a chance to use you, for the battle is not yours, it's the Lord's.

There is no sadness that Jesus can't feel, and there is no sorrow that the master is not able and willing to heal. Remember that all things are not going to be all good. But they are going to work according to God's purpose and His Holy will.

No matter what, I mean no matter what you are going through, remember God sees all and He knows all. He is just using you, for the battle is not yours, it's the Lord's.

"And he said, 'Listen, all Judah and the inhabitants of Jerusalem and King Jehoshaphat; thus says the Lord to you, Do not fear or be dismayed because of this great multitude, for the battle is not yours but God's." {2Chronicles 20: 15}

There is power in the name of Jesus to break every chain.

You are not entangled again with the yoke of bondage of chains. Jesus is the key you are looking for. Chains are broken and you can experience freedom in Christ Jesus.

Everyone in the body of Christ is manifested in the life of a sinner, the power of sin is broken and righteousness takes effect.

When Christ is manifested in the life of one who is bound, the chains are broken, and deliverance takes place. When He is manifested in your life, everything that is of darkness is dispelled.

Now that you are born again, the life in you is the supernatural life of Christ. Christ has fully tabernacled in you.

You have become His living headquarters. He looks through your eyes and walks with your legs because you have become His vessel, His body.

Chains are breaking and captives are set free, we are victors both in public and in our private spaces; actually, wherever we are, in Christ Jesus, chains are broken.

The truth of Jesus breaks every chain.

"And *you shall* **know** *the truth, and the truth shall make you free.*" {John 8:32}

When you are in Christ Jesus, you are no longer held down. You have arrived at a place of freedom, of which that is your

New Start, and it is with perseverance you have to keep moving, no longer allowing any chains past or present to bind you.

Now, it is easier to break physical chains and free individuals that are held captives against their will.

It is more difficult to cut people loose from mental chains they have helped to put them there. But difficult as it is, it has to be done.

If you desire to live and be all that God has spoken over your life in His word.

To do this requires another sort of liberation in which individuals are not only freed but also have their self- worth restored.

When people disappoint you, when they are disappointed in you, are when you may not even know why you feel the way you do. Remember! God will break away the chains that are stopping the flow in your life.

God is not the author of confusion and He will break away anything that may be holding you back. The Lord uses man to fulfil his purposes. Let us look at this scenario, and see how the Lord work his purpose using man.

A young man working in the Army, was constantly humiliated because of who he was and because of his belief in God. One day the captain decided to humiliate him more before the troop members in the camp, he called the young man and said:

'Young man, take the key and park the jeep aside.'

The young man replied, 'Sir I don't know how to drive, so I can't park the jeep.'

The captain said, 'Then ask for assistance from your God that you worship and show us that He exist.'

The young man cried, took the key and went to the vehicle praying to his God all the way....., and get into the car started it and moved it to a place where he was ordered and he parked the car perfectly well as the Captain wanted. The young man came out of the vehicle thanking his God.

To his surprise, he saw all the troops in his base who were watching and witnessing this; they were crying. They all said together to him, 'We want to serve your God!'

The young soldier was astonished, he wanted to know what was going on. The Captain was crying too, and he opened the hood of the jeep and showing it to the young man that the car had no engine in it.

The young soldier said, 'See, this is the God I serve, the God who gives life to what does not exist.'

You may think there are things that are still impossible, but in Jesus Christ, the Lord, the God of possibilities will be your God and the battles you are facing will be his battles. The battle is the Lord's, it is the Lord's my dear friend. Just hold your head up high.

You belong to the Most High God, and you don't need to cry as if there is no hope, no matter what you are going through, Remember; it's going to be alright; He's just using you.

God is only using you for He's worthy. He needs a chance to prove to your enemies that He is God. So what you have to do is to hold on. Don't give up. It's the Lords battle not yours.

"I am the Lord, the God of all mankind. Is anything too hard for me? "

{Jeremiah 32:27}

"Because thou hast made the Lord, which is my refuge, even the Most High, thy habitation. There shall no evil befall thee, neither shall any plague come high thy dwelling. For he shall give his angels charge over thee, to keep thee in all thy ways" {Psalms91:9-11}

All that is needed is to be in a right position with God and hold it tight to Him, people want and expect a lot about a lot in the Lord whereby they are not in a right position and are not holding it tight with God the maker of heaven and the earth.

POSITION YOURSELF

Most of the people claim to know God. Well that is fine and good, but the question is, despite of knowing God, have they seen God in a personal perspective of their lives? I mean one on one!

"Then the Lord said, "There is a place near me where you may stand on a rock." {Exodus 33:21}

Some people they come to the recognition and awareness of knowing and seeing God in their lives through some experiences they have undergone in their lives.

"In the year that King Uzziah died, I saw the Lord seated on a throne, high and exalted, and the train of his robe filled the temple" {Isaiah6:1}.

So even you, be in a good position in your spiritual life in order to face your battles and win them. Take the form of an Eagle.

The Eagle does not fight snake on the ground. It picks it up into the sky, and changes the battle ground and then it releases the snake into the sky.

Why?

The snake has no stamina, no power and no balance in the air. It is useless, weak and vulnerable unlike on the ground where it is powerful, wise and deadly.

Take your fights into the spiritual realm by prayer and fasting. There is no one that is more dangerous and powerful to the devil than someone who fasts and prays continuously. Not just once or on specific occasions, but continuously.

The devil will let you go free and never bother himself about you if you don't pray.

Why?

All because you are not a great harm or threat to him and his kingdom. But should you be someone who position yourself, and live a life style of prayer and fasting, it is then that you are strong and powerful to him.

That is why the devil does not allow many of us as Christians to go on fasting and prayer, the devil can allow you to pray and go and come to the Church and hear powerful sermons about God and Jesus Christ the Lord.

But when it comes to fasting the devil will do whatever it takes to discourage you not to go on fasting and prayer. There is proof that prayer and fasting harms the devil. To some bible manuscripts, you will not see this verse of Matthew 17:21; even if you see it, it doesn't directly state prayer and fasting.

Why?

Out of many verses, this is the only verse that tells and show us about prayer and fasting. The devil doesn't want you to see the value and power of prayer and fasting.

"Howbeit this kind goeth not out but by prayer and fasting." {Matthew 17:21}

So why and what stopping you to be in a right position? When you are in the Spiritual realm, God takes over your battles. You don't have to worry and fight them yourself.

Let us look at the last three sentences of verse 15; what did it say :

"......Do not be afraid or discouraged because of this vast army, for the battle is not yours, but God's" & **" You will not have to fight this battle. Take up your positions; stand firm and see the deliverance the Lord will give you, O Judah and Jerusalem. Do not be afraid; do not be discouraged. Go out to face them tomorrow, and the Lord will be with you"** {2Chronicles 20:15 & 17}

Don't fight the enemy in his comfort zone, change the battle grounds like the eagle, and let God take charge through your earnest prayers. Earnest prayer is so powerful, not just part time prayer but time and again

"Watch and pray so that you will not fall into temptation. The Spirit is willing, but the body is weak." {Matthew 26:41}

The above verse tells or warn us to watch and pray, so that we cannot fall into temptations. You know what? The devil will always tempt you and trick you even if you will claim that you are vigilante as the eagle.

The devil will whisper and tell you things in order to make you doubt your position and fall to its dirty schemes. The devil will play the mind games in your mind in order to confuse you and mislead your way of thinking.

BE VIGILANTE ALWAYS

"For though we walk in the flesh, we do not war according to flesh. For the weapons of our warfare are not carnal but mighty in God for pulling down strongholds." {2 Corinthians 10: 3-4}

The Battle is the Lord's

"Stand therefore, having girded your waist with truth, having put on the breastplate of righteousness, and having shod your feet with the preparation of the gospel of peace; above all, taking the shield of faith with which you will be able to quench all the fiery darts of the wicked one. And take the helmet of salvation and the sword of the Spirit, which is the word of God; praying always with all prayer and supplication in the Spirit, being watchful to this end with all perseverance and supplication for all saints." {Ephesians 6:14-18}

Today we pray to be spiritually aware, alert and vigilante as soldiers in our surroundings and atmosphere in Christ Jesus.

The enemy of our salvation is angry out there, and ready to attack and trick us anytime if we are not careful. Anyone in whom the Holy Spirit is not functional and not a believer in Christ Jesus is at risk.

The enemy is aiming to pull and defeat anyone on all levels: Physically, Mentally, Spiritually and Emotionally.

Be vigilante not only for yourself but for the others. Do not neglect any revelation from the Holy Spirit. Everyday anywhere, anytime, it's a war.

Look for warning signs and pray for that, before you enter any atmosphere even our churches. Enter in the Spirit as the children of Israel entered Jericho, so must you, each day.

Let praises be like war cries of victory in Jesus name. Our power is in our mouth. Our Armor is in the Spirit of our Lord Jesus Christ. Cover by the blood and fullness of the Glory and power of the Holy Spirit.

Let's live a life of not be misled by all means.

Let us look at this scenario, this is about the Snake and the Eagle. Here you will notice that the one is crawling on the ground, while the other is flying up high in the air. After you have read it, you will tell how the enemy the devil works and how it looks and think about you.

You will also learn how you, as the child of God, you should react when the enemy the devil attacks you.

While the Eagle was up high in the sky, it spotted the Snake crawling on the ground, the eagle flew down to it.

Eagle : I feel sorry for you snake, here you are doomed to crawl all your life. Not like me, I am destined to fly.

The Snake looked at the Eagle.

Snake : You are right Eagle, I can't fly, but only I who knows what it means to fly.

Eagle (laughingly) : But how can you know that? You don't have wings.

Snake (proudly) : Exactly that is what I thought you will say. Dreams are my heaven. While crawling on the ground, I close my eyes and I imagine that I am flying up high. In my free thoughts, I am learning to fly, with my soul and spirit through my faith I am rising high. So when my time comes and my life as a snake ends to this world, I will go to heaven and fly ,and not to think about anything except enjoying my freedom. And I won't be afraid to fly, because it won't be a new thing for me.

For you eagle, the wings you were given as you were born, but not for me. But heaven will make us equal. We will be flying together one day. I will be stronger and freer than you, all because I have learned how to fly without having wings, simply by crawling on the ground.

Both things are available for me, I am not afraid to lose my wings, because I know how to crawl, and I am not afraid to gain wings because I know how to fly.

But you eagle, what will you do if you lose your wings?

Let praises be like war cries of victory in Jesus name. Our power is in our mouth. Our Armor is in the Spirit of our Lord Jesus Christ. Covered by the blood and fullness of the Glory and power of the Holy Spirit.

Can you see that Spiritual faith of a snake? The snake never allowed the discouragements of the eagle, but the snake was positive and used the power of the tongue to protect itself from what the eagle was trying to do.

"Death *and life are in the power of the tongue, and those who love it will eat its fruit."* {Proverbs 18:21} &

"But **Jesus looked at them and said to them, 'With** *men this is impossible, but with God all things are* **Possible.'"** {Matthew 19:26}

Remember! This is one of the devil's deceptions and they come in many different forms, and because of lack of prayer and vigilante, many just surrender immediately from the devil deceptions.

You will be assured of clean victory. Pray without ceasing.

The devil will never tell you to be vigilante or to stay positive and faithful in your life. Instead he will whisper to you the only negative things that will mostly pull you down so you can see yourself as nobody. Here are the things that you should be vigilante and aware of, from the devil.

a) Devil will never tell you that you will be somebody.

b) The devil will never tell you that you will be successful.

c) The devil will never tell you that you will make it in your life.

d) The devil will never tell you that you should listen to God's advice.

The devil wants you to surrender and to remain where you are. You need to discover the purpose of God for your life.

For you to succeed in anything you are doing, you need to be vigilante. Jesus says in Matthew 10:16, "Behold, *I send you as a sheep in the midst of wolves. Therefore, be wise as a serpent and harmless as dove*".

Therefore! Be Sober and Vigilante.

Since you have been given knowledge about your number one enemy, the devil. He is roaring like a lion seeking whom he may devour or destroy. The word of God has given the children of God the strategies to overcome the enemy and his afflictions.

"Be *sober, be vigilant, because your adversary the devil walks about like a roaring lion, seeking whom he may devour. Resist him, steadfast in the faith, knowing that the same sufferings are experienced by your brotherhood in the world.*" { 1Peter 5:8-9}

That is to be sober and vigilante, resisting the enemy in the name of Jesus Christ. As a child of God, you have been called to be alert and enlightened in the word of God to know the tricks of the enemy so that you can stand against them in prayer and also make the right choices.

It is said that hard work beats talent, when talent doesn't work hard. And I do agree. After all; Talent is never just an innate ability. It's a lot more than just that. It's hard work, perseverance, discipline, vision, courage, faith, all are a bunch that is mixed up into one.

Know one thing: Hard work can take you high up in the ladder in your career.

HOLD IT TIGHT

When I grew up, I grew up under the parental guidance of my grandparents, me and my cousins. That is called an extended family. Basically, that is the life that we in the African community we are brought up to.

Our grandparents used to share with us some of the greatest stories of the events and the great man and woman in the history. And some fairy-tale stories.

But to me, there was this particular story that was shared by my grandmother, up to today, that story never left my mind. It kept on coming as I grow up.

The story happened long, long time ago, during the slavery times, when the Africans were forcedly taken and moved out of the African Continent through the ship, to be made slave in

The Battle is the Lord's

America, Europe and Asian continent.

It was discovered that among these slaves, there is this slave that was having in him a beautiful rare shiny stone. The voyager's tried to persuade this African young man to give them the stone.

But the young man refused to give them. So, what they did, they took the young man away from his fellow Africans, where the other slaves were kept in the lower basement of the ship.

He was taken to the upper base, to where the masters were, to eat and dine with them, he was receiving a very special treatment from his masters, because the master's wanted that stone; so they thought that by bringing him closer to them and lure him, he would finally give up and give them the stone.

The young African man, used to take out his stone from his pocket bag that was in his waist and played with it. When he was tired, he would go and get himself something to refresh. This went on and on, until there was this particular tragic sad day that led him to be taken back to the lower basement of the ship, where the other captured slaves were kept.

This happened when he was leaning over the curved stem post of the ship and was busy throwing his stone up and catch it and threw it up again. He kept on doing this as the ship was in motion in the middle of the deep ocean, until his precious stone fell down, deep in the middle of the ocean, that is how he lost his stone.

But today, this story made me realise that we the Christians, we have been entrusted with the precious big great things of God the father in heaven.

And the devil will do all his best to rob or steal to us what God has entrusted us with. We have to be very much cautious in what we do and strive to hold it tight what we have at all times. We have to safe guard what has been entrusted to us.

"Guard the good deposit that was entrusted to you--guard it with the help of the Holy Spirit who lives in us" { 2Timothy 1:14}

When it comes in holding tight to God, there is the story of a song writer Heratio Spafford, who wrote a famous well-known song: *"ALL IS WELL WITH MY SOUL."* It is so inspiring in knowing the things he went through and he had experienced. Let us look a bit to a short story of what he went through up to the point he wrote that song.

The writer was a successful Christian lawyer. Whom his only son died at age 4 in 1871. In 1872, the great Chicago fire wiped out his vast Estate made from his successful legal career. In 1878, He sent his wife and 4 daughters over to Europe on a summer trip on the ill-fated

SS Ville du Havre. Since he had a lot of work to do, he planned to follow them later.

The ship that have his family sank in the deep ocean. He lost his 4 daughters, with the wife that being the only survivor.

Of which she sent him a famous telegram which simply read: "SAVED ALONE". On his return home from visiting his wife in the hospital, his law firm was burned down and the insurance company refused to pay him. They said "It's the Act of God".

He had no money to pay for his house and no work, he also lost his house.

Then while sitting and thinking what is really happening to him, being a spiritual person, he wrote a famous well-known inspiring song: **"All is Well "**

These are the important motivating words that inspire me in that song:

"Whatever; my Lord, You have taught me to say- It is well, it is well with my soul."

So why don't you also, when things seem not to go well with you and also say to yourself it is well? Because by just saying those words, its motivating enough to stand still and face your battles and move forward.

What is it that takes your focus away from the things of God that makes you not to hold it tight to the Lord?

Is it your : **Work, *Finances*, Social life, Friends** or your *Family* ?

"Who shall separate us from the love of Christ? Shall trouble or hardship or persecution or famine or nakedness or danger or sword? " {Romans 8:35}

God did not bring you this far to leave you. No, not at all.

Our God does not do that. He never leaves nor forsake those who put their trust in Him.

You woke up this morning, asking God, Why your life is so messed up? Why nothing is going well for you. You beat yourself up for the past mistakes. You ask yourself a lot of "--*What if* --" questions?

Sometimes you wonder if you're the most cursed person. You ask what is it that you have done? That is not forgiven by God to prosper you.

Wait a minute right there!

Don't let the pressure upset you and make you uncomfortable. Hold it tight right there.

You woke up this morning out of bed, into your feet on the ground without any one's assistance, you stretched out your arms and yawned after a beautiful sleep of the night. Who gave you that privilege to wake up?

Yet! You are still saying you are cursed, you are not blessed, and who woke you up? Can't you see? The problem is with you.

You are failing to hold it tight to God's word and come to a realisation that waking up was the best gift of life and that each day is a blessing that can't be compared with anything.

We should learn to give thanks more than we ask and complain. You should hold it tight to God and his promises he had for us. God blesses everyone at His own time. He is never late or early. You cannot force His hand by whining and complaining. In everything, give thanks to the Lord. If not for anything.

Help Is At Hand

Let a man know what he wants to become. Let him hold on to this ideal and make it the blueprint that guides his work. This vision and the will to serve it, will mould the ultimate quality of our lives. It enables everyman to grow towards the image of his own dream.

Setting an exciting goal is like setting a needle in your compass from then on; the compass knows only one point, it's ideal. And it will faithfully guide you there through the darkest nights and fiercest storms.

Serious goal setters are like missiles with a target, because they have a specific destination, they can reach their potential. When the mind has defined target, it can focus and direct to it until it reaches its intended goal. It is not always easy to follow the proper course in life.

Sometimes our environment is not conducive and may even be frankly antagonistic to our dreams and Ideas. It is therefore unusual to find the major obstacles that may need to be overcome in order to succeed.

TRUST

Sometimes some situations that we find ourselves in may happen to look like it is the end of the world. Yet it is not, but it is a learning curve. Some things happen in our lives in order to learn, to teach us and to take us somewhere to another level that we did not even normally thought or realised that it will take us to a better level or position in our lives.

In fierce storms of the night or day, you will feel uncomfortable and not relaxed in the situation. It is then that you will need to look back deep down in your heart. At that particular moment you will discover that there is a hero in your heart.

Sometimes, God allows you to pass through some experiences to train your spirit to appreciate his love. Balaam never knew it was from God when he was angry with the donkey. Don't let your anger mislead and overcome you. Always put your trust in God totally, for He will turn the situation you are in for your own good.

"Then the Lord opened Balaam's eyes, and he saw the angel of the Lord standing in the road with his sword drawn. So he bowed low and fell face down. *The angel of the Lord asked him, "Why have you beaten your donkey these three times? I* *have come here to oppose you because your path is a reckless one before me. The donkey saw me and turned away from me these three times. If she had not turned away, I would certainly have killed you by now, but I would have spared her.* **Balaam said to the angel of the Lord, I have sinned. I did not realise you were standing in the road to oppose me. Now if you are displeased, I will go back.** *The angel of the Lord said to Balaam, 'Go with the men, but speak only what I tell you.'* **So Balaam went with the princes of Balak."** {Numbers 22:31-35}

All that is needed is courage, courage comes from trust. Trust is an unshakable belief in something or someone you know that will never let you down, even in good and in bad times.

Let us look at this scenario and see how man's trust and God's mysterious ways work.

One day, a local evangelist bragged during a crusade that his God was more able than all other god's in the town and the powers of the universe that the villagers worshipped when they are put together.

Just then when the rain storm started, The evangelist in the tent raised up his voice rebuking the rainstorm that it may not rain; and declared that if it rain, he won't consider himself as the man of God, and he urged also the people not to take him as a pastor anymore. He would stop preaching.

Before he could finish talking, it started to rain, and the people left the tent crusade in disappointment and dismay. The man of God was so disappointed and angry. He packed his belongings and left the town.

As he was in another town the next day at a shop to get himself something to drink, he went to a nearby park and set down drinking.

As he was sitting down, He was cursing God for such an

embarrassment He did to him. While he was seating and cursing God. Came to him an old man and tapped him gently on the shoulder, and said: **'Man of God'**, but the Evangelist quickly cut in.

"**Don't mention the name of God to me. He is fake, unreliable; I am no longer a believer in this God, what sort of a God is he, The God who chooses to disgrace his servants, leave me alone**"

But the Old man didn't listen to him, but continued to speak:

"**I am a relish priest in the village you just left, that you were preaching at. During your one week stay in that village; you destroyed all the charms I had made to the people of that village for over 45 years. Your prayers and your words always came with fearful fire and power. I tried so many times to eliminate you, but I could not My last chance came yesterday, I loaded my gun and went lying on the mountain top where I had a clear view of you and waited for you there. My plan was to shoot you from the distance since I could not get close enough to you due to the fire around you. But just when I lifted the gun; the rain you saw that came from nowhere yesterday, was wetting me and you were covered with clouds so that I could not even see you. All I saw was a bright man holding a sword in front of you. I was so terrified. I concluded that surely your God was indeed all powerful and mighty. That is why I've been looking for you, since then, because I** want to follow this God of yours."

The evangelist man of God, on hearing this, he bowed his head in shame, and started praying to God and cry for forgiveness of not trusting God.

"For the sake of his great name the Lord will not reject his people, because the Lord was pleased to make you his own" {1Samuel 12:22}

It's no wonder the scripture says:

"The Lord is good, a refuge in times of trouble. He cares for those who trust in him" {Nahum1:7}

God's solution is always in place before you even knew that there is a problem.

How I love this point!!! What are the things that shake you in trusting God?

- Is it Financial Worries?
- Conflicts with relatives?
- Concern about seeking first the Kingdom, while the boss demands you at work?

Remember! God has a solution in place even before you recognise the problem. We must learn to trust God and stop being anxious.

"Do not be anxious about anything, but in everything, by prayer and petition, with thanksgiving, present your requests to God" {Philippians 4:6}

Even if we suffer for doing what is right. Remember it is God who always allows the situations to happen to us, so that we will grow stronger.

In your lives, things may not always seem to go well and in the right direction as you are expecting. But you must never, *I mean* never lose your hope, because there is a great promise that was made for you. And the Lord God will never lie and turn his back against what He has promised to do for his people.

"Do not let your hearts be troubled. Trust in God; trust also in me "and "You may ask me for everything in my name, and I will do it." {John 14:1 and 14:14}

Today is always a great day to get faithful. God is always having a plan in place for you. If you will act with trust. God's timing is perfect.

"I am the Lord, the God of all mankind. Is anything too hard for me?" {Jeremiah 32:27}

A man of courage and trust; knows whom to turn and run to, that is God, because in Him, all things are possible. So what is it that keep people from living their lives and pursuing their dreams?

What is this element that causes so much anxiety and feeling of failure in people? I think you have already figured it out, that it is fear.

Immediately Jesus reached out his hand and caught him," You of little faith," He said, "Why did you doubt?" {Matthew 14:31}

And also the scripture says:

"Immediately the boy's father exclaimed,' I do believe, help me overcome my unbelief." {Mark 9:24}

Scripture above shows us that we have to ask our Lord Jesus Christ to help us to overcome our unbelief, it is our unbelief that makes things seems impossible to happen.

To put our trust in God and believe in Him, without this, our lives would be empty and our Christianity would be meaningless.

Don't you know that our lives are like popcorns, there is no way that we cannot trust God. Why am I saying we are like popcorns? Popcorn's are normally fried in the same pot in the same oil, at the same time and under the same heat conditions, but they do not all pop up at the same time.

When floods come, fish eat ants. When floods recede, ants eat fish. Only time matters. To make soap, oil is required. But to clean oil, soap is required.

Can you see what is the irony of life can be?

Everybody needs somebody at one point in time.

Do not despise or treat anyone with scorn. When they excelling or failing more than you. There is time for everything and for everyone. There is a miracle, when you believe, though hope is frail, it's hard to kill. Who knows what miracle you can achieve, when you believe, somehow you will, you will when you believe.

Keep trusting in God and waiting for your turn. Your time to pop will come at God's appointed time.

NEVER GIVE UP!!

BE TRUSTED

Let us look at this scenario. Several years ago, a preacher from a distant town accepted a call from a Church to another nearby town. Some weeks after his arrival, he had an appointment that made him board a bus to the other town.

When he sat down, he discovered that the driver had mistakenly given him extra change.

As he considered what to do, he thought to himself, "*You better give back the extra money*". Then another thought came, "*Oh, forget it, its only nothing, who will worry and notice this little amount?*"

After all the bus company makes a huge money on fares, they will never miss it. Accept it as a gift from God and keep quiet. When the preacher was getting down out of the bus, he paused a moment at the door and then handed the extra change to the driver and said. "Take the balance you gave me; it was over."

The driver, with a smile, asked the pastor, "Are you the new preacher in town?"

"Yes, I am", Pastor replied.

The driver said, "Well, I have been thinking a lot lately about where to go to worship. I just wanted to see what you would do if I give you extra change. Surely you have shown me that you are a trustworthy servant of God. I will go with you and worship your God at your Church."

When the preacher stepped off the bus, he grabbed a nearby pole, looked up and said, "Oh God; I almost sold your Son Jesus for just a change."

Our lifestyle is the only Bible that sometimes people can read. Your personal life, it's your true testimony. Here we see, how much people watch us as Christians. Remember, you are the light.

Therefore wherever you are people must see their hope, as you reflect God in Christ Jesus who is living in you.

"The people living in darkness have seen a great light; on those living in the land of the shadow of death a light has dawned " {Matthew 4:16}

"You are the light of the world. A city on a hill cannot be hidden " {Matthew 5:14}

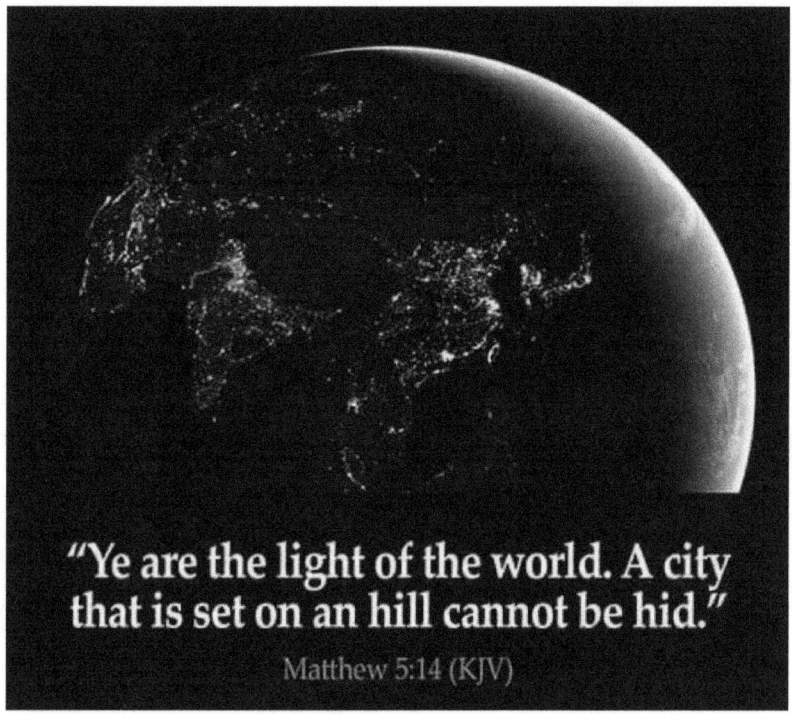

Remember that, people will put us to test.

Therefore, always be on guard and remember-you carry the name of Christ on your forehead and shoulders once you call yourself a Christian.

Therefore; watch your thoughts, they become Words. Watch your words, they became Actions. Watch your actions, they became a Habit. Watch your habit it becomes a Character; your character becomes your Destiny.

So whatever you do as a Christian, you are ministering to the outside world. Therefore, live a trustworthy life so you may not miss Heaven and not to be with our Lord my God Jesus Christ my Saviour.

FEAR

In a clear research that I have made on why people don't become successful in life, or don't reach to their desired destination, I have discovered that there is nothing else other than fear. What is it, this thing fear?

Fear is an ugly word that holds bad outcomes of the best life can offer. But what is it that they really fear?

Failure!!!

People want to avoid failure in their lives and go straight for success. They want to feel good and skip the bad altogether, so they want to avoid failure by throwing different situations into the fear.

"Ignoring what they said, Jesus told the synagogue ruler, "Don't be afraid; just believe". {Mark 5:36}

So how can you get past this fear?

"Therefore, my dear brothers, stand firm. Let nothing move you. Always give yourself fully to the work of the Lord,

because you know that your labour in the Lord is not in vain." {1Corinthians 15:58}

Paul here is clearly showing us that, we must give ourselves fully to the work of the Lord. We should not shift our position from the Lord, should we shift our position from the Lord, nothing, I mean nothing to whatever we do it will succeed, we will be labouring in vain.

Yes, I admit that there would be challenges along the way in your endeavours.

But let me tell you, challenges are good for the leader, challenges are good for the dreamer and you will not be successful in life without challenges. Challenges test your resolves.

It is probably true to say that no physical ailment can have a devastating effect upon a person as fear does.

Why do people feel this way ?

What do the words in the scriptures mean to us, whereby our Lord Jesus Christ tells us not to let our hearts to be troubled, but we have to believe in God and also in him.

So, what is it that keep people holding on to their fears?

"Do not let your hearts be troubled. Trust in God, trust also in me". {John 14:1}

The only means of overcoming this fear is to put your absolute trust in God.

"It is better to take refuge in the Lord than to trust in man". {Psalm 118:8}

This may appear to be too difficult and impractical.

"Why are you downcast, O my soul? Why so disturbed within me? Put your hope in God, for I will yet praise him, my Saviour and my God." {Psalm 43:5}

As you invite the Spirit of God in your life to strengthen your faith and as you open up your heart to Jesus.

"Whoever believes in me, as the Scripture has said, streams of living water will flow from within him. By this he meant the Spirit, whom those who believed in him were later to receive. Up to that time the Spirit had not been given, since Jesus had not yet been glorified " {John 7:38-39}

You will experience a sense of comfort and encouragement leading to you being filled with the peace that passeth all understanding.

It takes courage to walk into an atmosphere that is set against you. However, if you are going to get what you want out of life, out of God or any adverse situation, you've got to be prepared.

People may be murmuring in corners, but you have to know that the mission you are at it. Is so important that you cannot afford even to worry about what people think.

You must go anyway!

HONESTY

The first step in achievement of any goal is honesty. Be honest with yourself. This is true in becoming successful. Before you start any journey of self-improvement and during that journey, it is vital that you occasionally take the time intersection and self-analysis.

"Suppose one of you wants to build a tower. Will he not first sit down and estimate the cost to see if he has enough money to complete it? *31* **Or suppose a king is about to go to war against another king. Will he not first sit down and consider whether he is able with ten thousand men to oppose the one coming against him with twenty thousand?,&** *33* **In the same way, any of you who does not give up everything he has cannot be my disciple"** {Luke 14:28,31 &33}

This means taking a good long look in the mirror and making note of where you really are right now and determining how you are going to get where you want to go. Focus on that. Yes! In Christ everything is possible, but in order to achieve, you must know what you want.

"Therefore, my dear friends, as you have always obeyed-- not only in my presence, but now much more in my absence--continue to work out your salvation with fear and trembling" {Philippians 2:12}

Stop watering things that were never meant to grow in your life. What works, what's good, what's right, focus on it. Stop playing around with those dead bones and stuff you can't fix. It's over, leave it alone. You are coming into a season of greatness.

"Do not store up yourselves treasures on earth, where moth and rust destroy, and where thieves break in and steal. But store up for yourselves treasures in heaven, where moth and rust do not destroy, and where thieves do not break in and steal." {Matthew 6:19-20}

If you water what is alive and divine, you will see a harvest glooming like never before. Stop wasting water on dead issues, relationships, dead people and a dead past.

"He said, "Throw your net on the right side of the boat and you will find some." When they did, they were unable to haul the net in because of the large number of fish." {John 21:6}

You must be realistic with yourself.

"For by your words you will be acquitted, and by your words you will be condemned." {Matthew 12:37}

The scriptures in the book of Revelations 3:15 says, I know your deeds, that you are neither cold nor hot. I wish you were either one or the other! God doesn't like lukewarm people, if you are lukewarm, God won't be able to help you.

In reality what does that mean?

It means that in order to be successful in life, you must not be the jack of all trades, or else you will never know where you are going, and you will not have a focus.

Paul wrote a note or a letter to Timothy his spiritual son in the Lord, encouraging him to guard what was entrusted to him. Paul was highly aware that if you don't focus and you are not honest with yourself, you will lose what you have.

"Timothy, guard what has been entrusted to your care. Turn away from godless chatter and the opposing ideas of what is falsely called knowledge "

{1Timothy 6:20}.

So focus and Honesty are very important to each and every work, and the journey that you want to take. Let's say you want to go into a certain direction, like starting your own business. You have to take your time to check your progress in that direction and determine your greatest weakness. You know what? You are not totally helpless, because you know some few techniques on running the business and you haven't seen any serious limitations in your direction.

Do you know what? A bird sitting on a tree is never afraid of the branch breaking. Why? All because its trust is not on the branch but on its wings. Always believe in yourself.

You are honest in yourself, and you decide to get some training to improve yourself.

Good Move!

Then here comes now as time goes by and one day you notice that you have not taken any further steps forward.

"As Jesus went on from there, two blind men followed him, calling out, 'Have mercy on us, son of David!" {Matthew 9:27-28}

The truth is, you didn't take time to go and look for some help and advice, you just think about it, and you notice that you are still hesitating.

What is it that keeps you from making a simple telephone call to the ones who are much experienced and successful to you? It is that constant feeling that is happening inside you.

In the book of Acts10:2-4, it shows us that Cornelius found favour in God. Through the things he had done for others and humbleness and faithfulness he had showed to God, he was heard in his prayers. He was always turning to the one who could help him, asking him through prayers, because prayer changes things. Things that seems impossible, they become possible to God.

So what about you? Are you avoiding taking action towards your goal, because somewhere inside you, possible deep within your subconscious you believe that moving forward, it's impossible for you, and you know what?

This is where Honesty comes in again.

First and foremost, you must be honest with yourself <u>about your weaknesses</u>. And secondly, you must be honest <u>about the fears</u> associated with overcoming the weakness. And remember what the word says about you.

So if you believe that there is nothing, I mean nothing, you cannot do through Christ who strengthens you. Really, you can do almost everything in Christ Jesus.

If you do not take steps to recognize your fears, you will never be able to take any action and move towards your goals. So how can you be able to reach to your goal to please God who is not even seen by the eyes of the flesh, if you cannot be even be able to be honest even to yourself?

So stop and think about this logically, what are you afraid of? What could it be? Are you afraid of new environment, your success? That doesn't make sense. You find yourself in new environments all the time.

Your real fear is that you don't want to be humiliated.

You are afraid that you will look and appear bad in front of the others at this new environment. You are afraid to be a beginner because the others will look and laugh at you and make fun of your lack of skills and information. You don't like to be humiliated, so something within you has kept you from that environment.

After more thoughts, you decide this is no way to live your life. You do not want your life to be directed by fears; so you decide that you have to do something about the situation.

You have just done what very few will do in this life. You have taken the time honestly to recognize your fears and decided that you want to overcome those fears. CONGRATULATIONS!

Now here comes the hard part. You must take the final step and face your fears. Identifying and deciding to do away with your fears is easy as compared to actually confronting the situation of which you are afraid of it.

This will help to require courage and commitment. You must commit yourself to whatever you want to do to the Lord, and have a courage to follow through regardless of how much the situation you are faced with.

"Commit to the Lord whatever you do and your plans succeed." {Proverbs 16:3}

That's what make so many people fail to what they are doing because they go according to their wisdom, they don't enquire from the Lord to guide them.

"How can I give you up, Ephraim? How can I hand you over, Israel? How can I treat you like Admah? How can I make you like Zeboiim? My heart is changed within me; all my compassion is aroused. I will not carry out my fierce anger, nor will I turn and devastate Ephraim. For I am God, and not man---the Holy One among you. I will not come in wrath" {Hosea 11:8-9}

God is grieving and crying for the best things for us, His heart is on us. All we need to do is to have a courage to come closer to Him.

Remember; courage is not the absence of fear, but the ability to stand up and act even though you are fearful, to be courageous, face your fears and something will happen.

No matter what your problems or difficulties may be, once you seek the Lord in prayer and fasting, and relinquish yourself to Him, you will experience clarity of thought and a vision above all peace of mind.

In the book of Corinthians, we saw Paul crying for help to God, after the difficult experiences he has encounter, and what

Paul did, he ran to seek the help of the Lord, and the Lord God comforted him and said:

"My grace is sufficient for you, for my power is made perfect in weaknesses." {2Corinthians 12:9-10}.

Surely God says the same about you. So what more do you want, because help is at hand. Whatever failure you may come across with in your endeavours, that may want you to be discouraged, do not allow them to blind you to your future.

For your help is at hand.

"My son, if you accept my words and store up my commands within you, turning your ear to wisdom and applying your heart to understanding, and if you look for it as for silver and search for it as for hidden treasure, then you will understand the fear of the Lord and find the knowledge of God. For the Lord gives wisdom, and from his mouth come knowledge and understanding. He holds victory in store for the upright, he is a shield to those whose walk is blameless, for he guards the course of the just and protects the way of his faithful ones. Then you will understand what is right and just and fair---every good path. For wisdom will enter your heart, and knowledge will be pleasant to your soul.

Discretion will protect you, and understanding will guard you. Wisdom will save you from the ways of wicked men, from men whose words are perverse." {Proverbs 2:1-12}

You may have done things that are not pleasing and don't make God happy, in your consciousness, you may think that you don't deserve any more chance or any favour from the Lord. NO! It is not like that.

Don't even think of drifting back from serving God, but get rid of the things that separate you from the Lord.

"Do not be afraid," Samuel replied. "You have done all this evil; yet do not turn away from the Lord, but serve the Lord with all your heart." {1Samuel 12:20}

Because of His name's sake, God values his name up to the point that He will do whatever it takes to save his own people from destruction, as long as they are repenting and coming back to their senses that they have done wrong.

God does not hold or judge people on their past, or what they have done yesterday.

No; not at all. He is not like that; He is a gracious God.

We have to know that and have trust in Him. God loves a repenting sinner that acknowledges his or her sins, just like a saint. So there is no way that God can hold you on your past if you have confessed and repented. Because God is a forgiving father. It is your sins and your works that will judge you and condemn you.

Be Cautious

Christianity is not an easy life to live, but it is the best life that anyone can live in his life time. Why am I talking like this?

"But small is the gate and narrow the road that leads to life, and only a few find it." {Matthew 7:14}

It changes nobody to be somebody.

Yes! I admit that being a Christian is very challenging. Satan will come left and right to see to it that you lose your divine relationship that you have with the Lord.

But all it takes is you and your convictions. When you have a strong conviction in you about your Christianity, you will be much more cautious in mind and watch your footsteps carefully.

You should not be easily impressed by anything that comes along your way and your surroundings. One thing that will make you grow and be strong in your convictions to the Lord, is to be obedient. Listen and do what the Lord God says or wants you to do as you are commanded by the Lord.

Unlike Jonah, who was sent to Nineveh. Instead, because of

his disobedience, he took the other route where he was not directed to go to. He took a route to Tarshish, of which that caused a problem for others. Because sometimes we tend to do things that at the end of the day will put others at risk. All because of our disobedience.

"But Jonah arose to flee to tarshish from the presence of the Lord. He went down to Joppa and found a ship going Tarshish; so he paid the fare, and went down into it, to go with them to Tarshish from the presence of the Lord. But the Lord sent out a great wind on the sea, and there was a mighty tempest on the sea, so that the ship was about to be broken up." {Jonah 1:3-4}

Jonah thought he was wise, ran and hid himself, thinking that he won't be found by God. He had forgotten that the Lord my God is everywhere anytime, and He saw all our movements and actions. We cannot hide from God.

If God says "No", He doesn't want this from you to do, and you act as if you are innocent, you go and do as he asked you not to do. You will face the consequences.

Remember! Your sins will follow you!

If you look at King Saul, He was followed by his sins.

"But Samuel said, what then is this bleating of sheep in my ears? What is this lowing of Cattle that I hear?" {1Samuel 15:14}

God summoned Saul to go and destroy everything. We have to destroy. Yes, to destroy everything that the Lord doesn't want out of us. Our problem is that, we don't destroy everything. We have things that we are still keeping for our own benefit, and at the end of the day, they separate us from the Lord.

"Now go, attack the Amalekites and totally destroy everything that belongs to them. Do not spare them; put to death men and woman, children and infants, cattle and sheep, camels and donkeys "{1Samuel 15:3}.

We can lie with almost everything to everyone, with all the pretense that everything is alright, but not to God the Holy Spirit. We have to remember that the Holy Spirit searches all things, nothing is hidden to Him.

"But God hath revealed them unto us by his Spirit: for the Spirit searched all things, yea, the deep things of God " {1Corinthians 2:10}

That is what we saw to a man by the name Ananias and his wife, when they lied to the Apostles, when they said that what they brought forward is what they got when they sold some of their belongings. That is what the Christians of today are also doing to one another, forgotten that the very same brother they are lying to. Do also have the Spirit of the Lord in him.

"Now a man named Ananias, together with his wife Sapphira, also sold a piece of property. With his wife full of knowledge, he kept back part of the money for himself, but brought the rest and put it at the apostle's feet " 9 **"Peter said to her, "How could you agree to test the Spirit of the Lord? Look! The feet of the men who buried your husband are at the door, and they will carry you out also."** {Acts 5:1-2&9}

Therefore! In order to stay cautious and not fall to be the victim of the devil, you have to avoid to do what is evil and do what is right.

"Avoid every kind of evil." {1Thessalonians 5:22}

In life, I have learned some painful lessons about cautiousness and the importance of being carefully considering how my actions might impact my future.

In our Spiritual daily lives, we need to take good care of ourselves, If we expose ourselves foolishly, that could lead us to danger and became easy targets. What is it that is sacred in us? Christ Jesus, we have to look after it.

"Do not give dogs what is sacred; do not throw your pearls to pigs. If you do, they may trample them under their feet, and then turn and tear you into pieces." {Matthew 7:6} And

"Dear friends, do not believe every spirit, but test the spirits to see whether they are from God, because many false prophets have gone out into the world." {1John 4:1}

This is one of the serious warnings that we are being told. Not to believe every spirit, but to test the spirits. Off which that is a serious problem we are encountering and experiencing in these days, and also out there in the world, we are seeing a number of false prophets. And to be in a safe position, we should know and identify how God speaks to us. God speaks in different ways and it is important to be aware of these ways. We should ask ourselves if we are truly listening to Him. In order for us to listen, it's vital that we not only hear Him speak, but we listen to how He speaks.

How God Speaks?

There are a number of ways in which God can speak to His people. He can speak through circumstances, wise counsel, dreams, and visions, our thoughts, natural and supernatural manifestations and through prophets. As His people, we should be able to identify True and False prophets.

HOW PROPHETS MANIFEST (WORK)

Many confuse Prophets and men with the gift of prophecy. Prophets are born prophets, but as for the gift of prophet, we receive it through faith. Everyone can have the gift of prophecy, but not everyone who prophesises are Prophet.

Prophecy is a gift of prophecy that needs two or three witnesses in Church, not a Prophet. A Prophet does not ask to prophesy or seek permission or approval in Church.

It is the gift that we don't control as a Church or the one who prophecies. It is not anyone's will or the Church. It just happens because the man is led and controlled by the move of the Holy Spirit within him, to speak what the Lord God want them to say.

Prophets serve as the eyes and mouth piece of the Church, and they also stand between men and God to speak from God. Prophets of God are mostly needed in these last days. If we say we don't believe in prophecy in our Churches, or fail to accept Prophets, or fail to give them their proper positions, we are fooling ourselves and stand against the will of God my Lord.

It makes no sense at all for a Prophet to go to a Bible school that works according to the will and doctrine of man not God's will. There is no Bible school at all for the Prophets of God.

"Did the word of God originate with you? Or are you the only people it has reached?" {1Corinthians 14:36}

Yes! There can be Bible schools for prophets, but those prophets will not be working according to the plan and will of God, but according to what the doctrine of men has taught them to do, not what God wants them to do.

These Bible school prophets ruin and delay the work of God's will and plan about men on earth. We have a teacher that is the Holy Spirit. He alone is enough to guide and teach us of what we have to do or not. Going to Bible school doesn't make you a real true minister of the word of God. But only God who makes man to be a true minister.

"How, then, can they call on the one they have not believed in? And how can they believe in the one of whom they have not heard? And how they can hear without

someone preaching to them? And how can they preach unless they are sent? As it is written, 'How beautiful are the feet of those who bring good news.'" {Romans 10: 14 - 15}

Going to Bible school actually is for your own benefit, you are not doing God any favour. Actually, it's you who needs Gods favour and help. Many people have fallen the victims of false prophets out there.

We should ask Jesus Christ, who is the author of Prophecy, to help us through the power of the Holy Spirit to have a Spiritual eye to see and analyse what is happening and being prophecies.

"Two or three prophets should speak, and the others should weigh carefully what is said." {1Corinthians 14: 29}

God is present in our lives. Prophecy is an indication that God is present in our lives. Being in contact with a true prophet means your life will never be the same again.

DIFFERENT TYPES OF PROPHETS:

- **Ro'eh :** The word Ro'eh means a seer. Ro'eh prophets can see, but are not allowed to speak on certain platforms.

- **Chozeh :** Chosen prophets can see and talk.

- **Massa :** Massa means burden and it reveals the response of the one receiving God's message.

- **Naba :** Naba means to bubble up, gush forth or pour forth. Naba prophets are not trained, but have something flowing out of their bellies.

- **Nataf:** These prophets are born with the prophetic gift and are skilled.

FALSE PROPHETS

- **An Observer of times**: An observer of times is a false prophet who makes predictions from the reading of clouds and even water.

- **A Witch**: A witch makes use of supernatural forces, They are associated with magic and often make predictions.

- **A Charmer**: A charmer is a person who ties others into knots, mystifying them with what they are saying.

- **A Consulter**: A consulter consults and channels a spirit of medium.

- **A Wizard**: Wizards claim wisdom from something other than human sources. They deal directly with demons.

- **A Necromancer**: A necromancer is one who communicates with the dead. They are similar to the consulter.

A number of Christians are not cautious, they have fallen to a number of traps, that even led them to confusion in their Spiritual lives and ended up not serving the Lord the way they are expected to do so. They are not worshipping God the way He wants to be worshipped. Even the elect are misled.

"For false Christ and false prophets will rise and will show great signs and wonders, so as to misleàd, if possible, even the elect." { Matthew 24 :24 }

Why?

Because along the way, they have come across a number of teachings that led them astray. If you look at the scriptures above, it warns us to be cautious, unlike the prophet, the man of God in the book of 1Kings; whereby he was ordered by God not to eat or drink, and not to use again the very same route he has used when he was returning from where he was ordered by God.

"For I was commanded by the word of the Lord: '*You must not eat bread or drink water or return by the way you came.*" So he took another road and did not return by the way he had come to Bethel." {1Kings 13:9-10}

Though the man of God the prophet was highly aware of what God said to Him, but he was not cautious and he was easily misled by the old prophet, because the man of God believed him. He did not enquire from the one who has ordered him before, and see if this old man, what he is saying, is it really true; is it something that come from the Lord, who had ordered him in the first place.

What this man of God encountered and experienced is what most of the Christians encounter and find themselves in it. They don't enquire from the Lord who has called them and who have ordered themselves.

They tend to listen to other people most of the time; I'm not saying people must not listen to others, but be cautious.

"Her prophets whitewash these deeds for them by false visions and lying divinations. They say, 'This is what is the Sovereign Lord says'---when the Lord has not spoken." {Ezekiel 22:28}

But they must be careful when it comes to the things of the Lord, especially when the Lord God has spoken directly to them in the first place. Even though they are aware of what the bible says and its warnings to them, they are not cautious. But they tend not to go according to it.

"Watch out for false prophets, they come to you in sheep's clothing, but inwardly they are ferocious wolves. {Matthew 7:15}

IDENTIFYING A WOLF IN SHEEP'S CLOTHING

In every day of life that you live, you meet different characters of people. Some with good, some with bad attitudes and different agendas. Well that is the nature of a human being. Out of all that, some that you come across with, you will easily identify their true colours. Some, you won't even manage to identify them, they hide their true identity to you, those are the wolves.

Sometimes you will notice that they are sly, they get away with things by playing with other people's emotions, lying and manipulative. One thing is for sure, a wolf in sheep clothing is good at hiding their true intentions. They are secretive and mostly they are unpredictable.

I believe by now in your mind you have someone that stuck and you are thinking of who relates to this. Someone you don't get him/her exactly who she/he is.

Well that person may not be the one. The wolf in sheepskin is someone you don't even think of that can be. So don't let your mind mislead you. Be wise and vigilant. Well here we will pull out the wool over your eyes, and look out for the signs of a wolf in sheepskin, so that next time, you will tell me if you have not identified the wolf in them. And you will not be awake and aware.

WOLF IN SHEEPSKIN SIGNS:

a) ***Plays with others***: Emotional, Spiritually, and Physically. They are so manipulative. They will engage you in things that will benefit them at the end of the day. They gather around people they can be in control of them.

"Be sober, be vigilant; because your adversary the devil walks around like a roaring lion, seeking whom he may devour." {1Peter 5:8}

b) ***Sweet talk:*** Everything they say it looks and seems real and possible in so much that you will believe them and fall to their trap and agenda. They make things to be too good to be true, for their own personal gain at the end of the day.

"Watch, stand fast in the faith, be brave, be strong " {1Corinthians 16:13}

c) ***They Act***: They appear to be too much caring, concerned and worried about you. Until you fall in building trust and form a bond with them. That is where you will end up being an easy target of them, that is deception.

"And No wonder! For Satan himself transforms himself into an angel of light. Therefore it is no great thing if his ministers also transform themselves into ministers of righteousness, whose end will be according to their works " {2Corinthians 11:14-15}

d) ***Don't take critics***: They always want to appear as they are the best in whatever they are doing. When they do something, they don't want to be confronted. They don't feel comfortable with people who will not agree and do things in their own way. They don't want to be criticized and be corrected.

"Open rebuke is better, than love carefully concealed. Faithful are the wounds of a friend, But the kisses of an enemy are deceitful " {Proverbs 27:5-6}

e) ***They Look Troubled***: Wolf in sheep's clothing tend not to smile as much as people who live authentically and tell the truth no matter what consequences. There is huge strain in their conscience and consequently makes them feel like they have two tons of bricks weighing down on them. In them, you will notice that they don't really have much emotion. Stories eventually eat people up on the inside, and their usual temperament is a telling sign of how they really feel.

HAVE SELFISH HIDDEN MOTIVES

a) *Body Language*: You will notice some unusual body language and eye contact is not stable. They will even try to force starring at you as they believe that it will prove them trustworthy.

b) *Negative Emotions*: The other way to spot some with hidden motives is by how they make you feel. Your own negatives emotions towards them are a warning sign to you that something isn't feeling right in your gut. You should trust your guts in regard to someone with hidden motives.

c) *Same thing as you*: You will notice them that they are not encouraging and motivating you towards your plans. Instead, when you desire something, they will always have the same desire as you do to that very something you are also focusing and having interest to it. To spot them, try as many times as you can to change the subject as much as many times; and you will notice their reactions.

d) *Persuade You*: They will always try and test your

vigilance by keeping on being persuasive. They will try and do their best to persuade you in order to fulfil their hidden motives. Be watchful. Persuasion is a useful skill to use when you are in need of something, not against you.

REMEMBER!

So, in order for you to be on safe side of a wolf in sheep's clothing:

1) Be Watchful;

2) Know the real and you will know the fake too;

3) Know God's word, that will make you to be easy to know when the word of God is twisted and manipulated;

4) Lean on wisdom of God's Spirit living in you, and always seek God's guidance to stand firm.

"Where there is no counsel, the people fall; But in the multitude of counsellors there is safety." {Proverbs 11:14 }

Let's not waste time fighting against ourselves, but recognize who the real enemy is. Wolves in sheeps' clothing or the false prophets, they can totally be misleading if you are not aware and awake.

"The old prophet answered, "I too am a prophet, as you are. And an angel said to me by the word of the Lord: 'Bring him back with you to your house so that he may eat bread and drink water' " (But he was lying to him) .**So the man of God returned with him and ate and drink in his house."**{1Kings 13:18-19}

And what the Bible says, does it not say that we must test the Spirits?

"Dear friends, do not believe every spirit, but test the spirits to see whether they are from God, because many false prophets have gone out into the world."{1John 4:1}

Let us observe or see what these different types of false prophets are and how they perform their duties. So that we can see when the word of God warns us to test the spirits if they are from God talks about.

Yes, it says so and that is where the prophet of God failed to do and that is what happens to the most of the Christians. They are not cautious, they are easily taken and impressed by all sorts of strange teachings.

"Do not be carried away by all kinds of strange teachings. It is good for our hearts to be strengthened by grace, not by ceremonial foods, which are of no value to those who eat them " {Hebrews 13:9}

As a Christian, you have to be cautious and be on your guard and not find yourself losing your position in the Lord. And fall to traps of the devil.

"Many deceivers, who do not acknowledge Jesus Christ as coming in the flesh, have gone out into the world. Any such person is the deceiver and the antichrist. Watch out that you do not lose what you have worked for, but that you may be rewarded fully " {2John 7-8} and

"Therefore, dear friends, since you already know this, be on your guard so that you may not be carried away by the error of lawless men and fall from your secure position." {2Peter 3:17}

And what were the outcomes of not being cautious, the man of God found himself in danger that led him even to death, why it ended like that?

It is because when we are not cautious of ourselves, in our

spiritual lives, the Lord distances himself from us, especially when He had warned and spoken to us. We became easy targets.

"When the prophet who had brought him back from his journey heard of it, he said, It is the man of God who defied the word of the Lord. The Lord has given him over to the lion, which has mauled him and killed him, as the word of the Lord had warned him " {1Kings13:26}

Can you see that now, the very same person who misled the man of God with all lies of sweet talk, when things have gone wrong with the man of God. What is this false old prophet is doing now? He is turning the whole blame to the man of God.

Can you see what we said earlier on about the wolf in a sheepskin that they have the sweetest talk, everything they say it looks and seems real and possible in so much that you will believe them and fall to their trap and agenda.

Therefore, what is needed is to be awake and be very selective.

"Those people are zealous to win you over, but for no good. What they want is to alienate you {from us}, so that you may be zealous for them. It is fine to be zealous, provided the

purpose is good, and to be so always and not just when I am with you." {Galatians 4:17-18}

Out there, the world is rough. It is not what it looks as it is, the devil is always looking for its prey. Let it not be you, who can be that prey and fall into the hands of the devil. It is no wonder we hear or see Paul writing to his spiritual son, warning him to be careful to his spiritual life and to watch himself carefully, or if he does so, he would have done himself and them a big favour. Of which that is what we really have to do.

"Watch your life and doctrine closely. Persevere in them, because if you do, you will save both yourself and your hearers." {1Timothy 4:16} and

"So then, let us not be like others, who are asleep, but let us be alert and self-controlled." {1Thessalonians5:6}

Commit To The Lord

Let God be the one who is in charge of your life and influences you in your daily living.

Yes, I admit that your family responsibilities and sometimes your family and friends will condemn you, but you know what the word says; there is no condemnation for those who are in Christ.

"Therefore there is no condemnation for those who are in Christ Jesus." {Romans 8:1}

Your work will demand a lot of your time, but you must grow and develop a strong backbone, stand tall and hold it tight to the Lord your God. Just hold your head up. You belong to the Most High God.

"All man will hate you because of me, but he who stands firm to the end will be saved "{Matthew 10:22} And

"I know where you live---where Satan has his throne. Yet you remain true to my name. You did not renounce your faith

in me, even in the days of Antipas, my faithful witness, who was put to death in your city---where Satan lives " {Revelations 2:13}

Yes! Things may not go as we expect them to be in our lives, but revitalise your faith again and again all the time. You have the Lord Jesus Christ and the Holy Spirit in you to achieve your goals and to overcome any obstacles and all the challenges that may come and stand on your way.

It's the determination and commitment to the Lord and an unswerving faith that will enable you to attain the success you seek.

Faith is the awareness that the creator is running the world and all that happens is for your ultimate benefit. The more faith you have, the more you will find yourself experiencing greater things in your inner peace and serenity.

I know one thing; Mountains can be huge and high and Rivers can be wide and deep, and as small as you are. All I know and believe is that, you can climb to those mountains and swim to those rivers.

"So then, those who suffer according to God's will should commit themselves to their faithful Creator and continue to do good " {1Peter 4:19}

God want to use those who lift up their hands and avail themselves to be used by him. Those who will be used by God as he used that donkey when he was about to enter Jerusalem.

"Saying to them, 'Go to the village ahead of you, and at once you will find a donkey tied there, with her colt by her. Untie them and bring them to me. If anyone says anything to you, tell him that the Lord needs them, and he will send them right away." {Matthew 21:2-3}

As that donkey was available to be used, so as you when you avail and commit yourself to the Lord my God, He will use you right away. For God wants those who are like that, who have their heart to Him.

When you are in Christ Jesus and you have hold it tight, you will maintain and experience a great freedom and relief in your life, in Christ when you are free, you are free indeed.

"It is for freedom that Christ has set us free. Stand firm, then, and do not let yourselves be burdened again by a yoke of slavery" {Galatians 5:1}

The only way that can help you as a child of the living God, is by wearing Gods Armor, you will go strong in the Lord.

Nothing can penetrate in you, His strong arm will get you into victory in the areas of your weaknesses, He will do marvellous things for you, His right hand and Holy arm will deliver you.

"Finally, be strong in the Lord and in his mighty power. Put on the full armour of God so that you can take your stand against the devil's schemes."

and

"Therefore, put on the full armour of God, so that when the day of evil comes, you may be able to stand your ground, and after you have done everything, to stand. Stand firm then, with the belt of truth buckled around your waist, with the breastplate of righteousness in place " {Ephesians 6:10-11 and

13-14}

You should do this in maintaining your life to the Lord and knowing that in challenges you are coming across with, the battle is not yours is the Lord's battle, and keeping in mind that help is at hand and the Lord is there at all times to help you because he is the refuge of those who earnestly seek Him.

You must be cautious at all times and define the target you want to reach and stay focussed to that intended goal. Under any circumstances, be cautious and stay alert in any interruptions and delays, never lose sight of your goal.

"Do not be afraid of what you are about to suffer. I tell you; the devil will put some of you in prison to test you, and you will suffer persecution for ten days. Be faithful, even to the point of death, and I will give you the crown of life " {Revelations 2:10}

You should do this leaning to the word of the living God, and if you do so, you will stand fitted to the ground in Christ Jesus.

"And with your feet fitted with the readiness that comes from the gospel of peace." {Ephesians6:15}

AMEN

"Never measure God's Power by your limited expectations."

Our God can do things for us more than we expect. Trust in Him, you will see and experience wonders of His work.

Luthando Ningiza

www.ingramcontent.com/pod-product-compliance
Lightning Source LLC
Chambersburg PA
CBHW032042040426
42449CB00007B/981